Put Down Your Phone

by Brandon C. Finch

Illustrated by
Brian Beausoleil

Put Down Your Phone

Copyright © 2017 Brandon C. Finch
All Rights Reserved

No part of this book may be reproduced in any manner
in any media, or transmitted by any means whatsoever, electronic
or mechanical (including photocopy, film or video recording,
internet posting, or any other information storage and retrieval system),
without the prior written permission of the publisher.

ISBN-13: 978-0692662533
ISBN-10: 0692662537
BISAC: Humor / Form / Pictorial

Printed in the United States of America

Published by
Brandon C. Finch
silencethealerts.com

M, forgive me for always being on my phone.
—*B*

Do you remember
back in the day?
When people talked
and kids would play?

Things have changed,
these times are new.
Your friends have noticed;
your loved ones, too.

I'll paint a picture, perhaps it's you?
It's not a pleasant image; it's not a pretty view.

Do you feel anxious, away from your phone?
Do you think when it's with you, you're never alone?

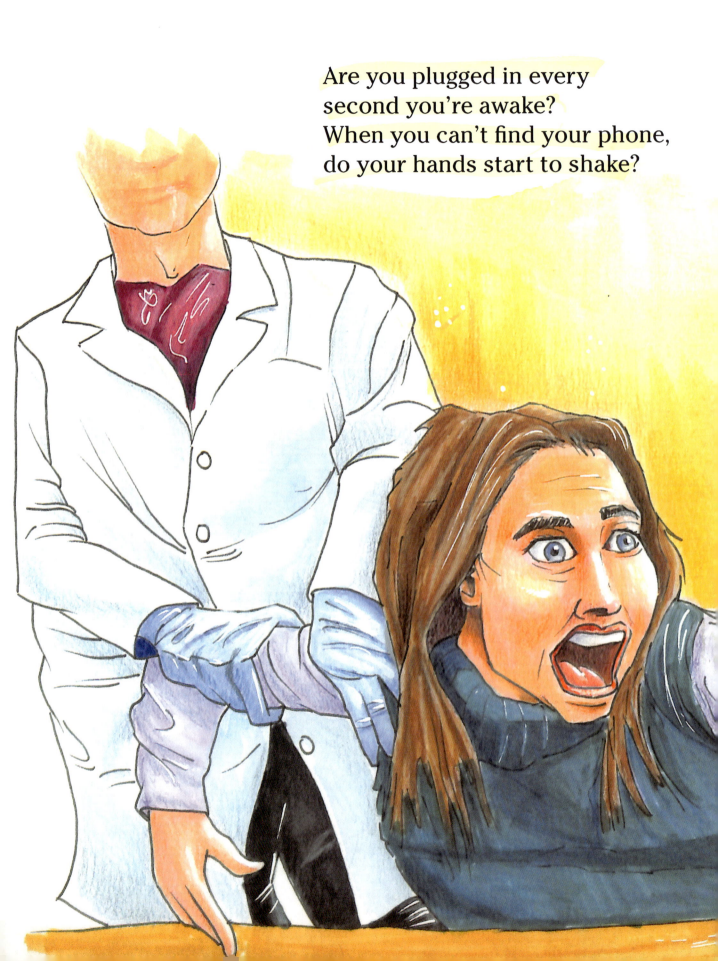

Glued to your device,
the addiction is clear.
I'm sure it's a phase,
you've nothing to fear.

Texting and walking, texting and driving,
Texting and drinking, and even skydiving?

Crushing candy, taking selfies, updates PING.
Our phones do everything, except RING!

Capture memories, chat and "check in."
Who needs people when your phone is your friend?

Every craving is there, no need to wait.
A pizza, a taxi, even a date!

From pictures, to games, it's all the rage.
Connection is COOL in the Digital Age.

Counting steps, playing tunes, and streaming shows.
Our phones make it easy for life on the go.

But forget to look up from your favorite device?
You'll find its convenience comes at a price.

The constant connection
can be a curse.
To your mind, your body,
your wallet or purse.

Emailing and tweeting and 'gramming, oh my.
To say this is normal would be a lie!

Phones have germs. They hinder your sleep.
The cost of upgrades can make you weep!

Remember when our fingers weren't numb?
Before "smart phones" made us all dumb?

We can have that again,
I promise we can.
It won't be easy but
follow this plan.

No phones at the table, that's where you eat.
I'm serious, I mean it; not even a tweet!

Please no phones on the toilet, let yourself be.
Have some dignity people; it's the place where you pee.

Using your phone at the checkout is rude. Cashiers are human, they have feelings too!

No calls at the gym, on a bus, or a train.
Not the movies, a meeting, or inside a plane.

Phones in the bed are frowned upon too.
A phone in the shower? What's wrong with you?

Put down your phone, how hard can it be?
Unless, of course, it's an emergency.

It's time for a change, so swallow your pride.
Unplug, detach, enjoy life's ride.

It's not *that* hard, there's so much to do.
Read a book, take a walk, learn something new!

So silence the alerts, get out and play.

A day without phones is a ~~damn~~ good day.

Made in the USA
Charleston, SC
03 January 2017